Accelerate Your Leadership

A Guide to Success in a New Role

James Royce Smartman

Copyright © 2024 James Royce Smartman

All rights reserved.

DEDICATION

To all the leaders who have the courage to embrace change, take on new tasks, and encourage others to follow in their footsteps. I hope your journey is full of the bravery to push boundaries, the knowledge to learn from every experience, and the resilience to succeed in every new role you embark on. May you always lead with integrity, passion, and vision. You should read this book.

CONTENTS

ACKNOWLEDGMENTS..1

CHAPTER 1...1

Recognizing Transition's Difficulties......................................1

    1.1 The Changeover A dilemma..1

    1.2 Typical Transitional Pitfalls..3

    1.3 The First Ninety Days Are Crucial..................................6

CHAPTER 2...10

Get Ready Before You Begin..10

    2.1 Evaluating Your Circumstance.......................................10

    2.2 Finding Important Stakeholders.....................................13

    2.3 Establishing Reasonable Goals......................................15

CHAPTER 3...19

Getting Results Early..19

    3.1 The Importance of Early Victories.................................19

    3.2 Determining Early Success Areas..................................22

    3.3 Putting Early Changes into Practice...............................24

CHAPTER 4...28

Acquiring Knowledge of the Terrain......................................28

    4.1 Performing Research in Organizations..........................28

    4.2 Internal Network Mapping..31

    4.3 Team Dynamics Analysis...34

CHAPTER 5...39

Getting Important Stakeholders to Support You Early........39

- 5.1 Establishing Connections with Superiors 39
- 5.2 Building Trust with Colleagues 42
- 5.3 Winning Direct Reports' Trust 45

CHAPTER 6 50
Matching Organizational Objectives with Vision 50
- 6.1 Outlining a Vision for Personal Leadership 50
- 6.2 Establishing Both Short- and Long-Term Objectives 52
- 6.3 Expressing the Goal 55

CHAPTER 7 60
Evaluating and Developing Your Group 60
- 7.1 Assessing the Strengths and Weaknesses of the Team 60
- 7.2 Formulating Team Member Development Plans 63
- 7.3 Selecting New Hires and Reassignments 66

CHAPTER 8 71
Implementing Efficient Procedures 71
- 8.1 Determining Important Operational Procedures 71
- 8.2 Simplifying the Process 75
- 8.3 Putting Process Improvements into Practice 78

CHAPTER 9 82
Establishing a Powerful Individual Brand 82
- 9.1 Building Trustworthiness 82
- 9.2 Highlighting Capabilities in Leadership 85
- 9.3 Regularly Assessing Yourself 87

CHAPTER 10 90
Long-Term Success Planning 90

10.1 Maintaining Initial Gains 90

10.2 Establishing a Framework for Continuous Improvement 93

10.3 Creating a Leadership Legacy 96

ABOUT THE AUTHOR 100

ACKNOWLEDGMENTS

I want to sincerely thank everyone who has helped to create **Accelerate Your Leadership** and who has been a part of this adventure.

I am very grateful to my family and friends for their constant belief in me, support, and encouragement. Throughout the many hours spent creating and perfecting this book, your understanding and patience have been invaluable.

I would also like to express my gratitude to my mentors and coworkers, whose knowledge and perceptions influenced a lot of the guidance presented here. I am really appreciative of the lessons you have taught me, and your advice has been a continual source of inspiration.

To the teams and leaders I've had the honor of working with, thank you for sharing your real-world experiences, which helped to root this book in reality. I now have a better knowledge of leadership and the human element in every choice thanks to your struggles and victories.

Finally, I want to express my gratitude to the reader for selecting this book. I hope the resources, knowledge, and tactics I've provided here enable you to further your leadership development and succeed long-term in any new position you take on.

We appreciate your confidence and dedication to your personal development.

CHAPTER 1

RECOGNIZING TRANSITION'S DIFFICULTIES

Making the move to a new position or setting is a complex process that involves both opportunities and difficulties. Transitions offer leaders an opportunity to introduce new ideas and encourage creativity. But they are also extremely vulnerable periods, when the stakes are enormous and mistakes could have long-term consequences. This chapter delves deeply into the intricacies of leadership changes, emphasizing the main obstacles, typical hazards, and the value of strategic planning in the crucial initial months.

1.1 The Changeover A dilemma

Transitions provide a special conundrum since they are both times when leaders are most at risk and times when innovation and progress are possible. Leaders must quickly adjust to a new corporate culture or team dynamic during this phase, deal with increased scrutiny, and fulfill the high expectations of their teams and stakeholders. It takes a combination of self-assurance, modesty, and smart thinking to navigate this balancing act.

- **Innovation Opportunities:** Phases of transition can serve as a blank canvas, enabling new leaders to make adjustments that might not have been possible in the past. Leaders have the opportunity to spot weaknesses, optimize procedures, and present game-changing concepts that could influence the organization's course.

- The team, senior management, and external stakeholders closely examine every choice made by a new leader, making them extremely vulnerable. Errors made during this time can damage trust, create a bad impression, and prevent success in the future. Therefore, leaders need to be careful and work hard to gain the trust of their new team.

Getting Used to New Teams and Cultures: Every organization has a distinct culture, and even within an organization, the dynamics, expectations, and values of each team might differ. To lead effectively, leaders need to be able to swiftly understand these subtleties. This includes:

- Team members' needs and priorities are understood by carefully listening to them.

- In order to prevent interfering with efficient procedures, it is important to observe current workflows and communication patterns.

- To establish rapport and learn about the team's areas of strength and improvement, an open discourse should be held.

1.2 Typical Transitional Pitfalls

Phases of transition are full of possible pitfalls. Leaders frequently make mistakes that result from a failure to build important relationships, an over-reliance on prior experiences, or a lack of awareness of the organization's culture.

Failing to Build Alliances: A leader's success depends on assembling a coalition of support within an organization. Even well-meaning reforms may encounter opposition in the absence of supporters and allies. Successful leaders actively look for:

- The team and organization's **key influencers** who have the ability to promote change.

- **Cross-functional partnerships** that can offer more comprehensive support and insights.

- **Mentors and advisors** who are able to provide direction and who are aware of the complexities of the organization.

The undervaluation of cultural dynamics One common mistake is not understanding and respecting the organization's cultural standards. Leaders who bring strict ideals or preconceived conceptions to a new setting may cause friction and alienate team members by clashing with the prevailing culture. Effective leaders devote time to education:

- There are **unwritten rules** that govern how the team interacts.

- Team conduct is influenced by shared beliefs and traditions.

- Conventions pertaining to decision-making, conflict resolution, and feedback.

Overemphasizing Immediate Results: In order to prove their worth, new leaders could feel under pressure to achieve quick victories. Although outcomes are crucial, placing too much focus on immediate benefits might backfire. Building a solid basis for future success and achieving early triumphs require leaders to find a balance. This comprises:

- Establishing achievable short-term goals that show proficiency without overburdening the group.

- In order to prevent a reactive attitude, immediate priorities should be in line with long-term corporate goals.

1.3 The First Ninety Days Are Crucial

Since they establish the tone for subsequent interactions and leave a lasting impression on stakeholders and team members, the first ninety days of a new leadership position are crucial. Carefully managing this phase allows leaders to build momentum, build credibility, and create a solid basis for long-term success.

The foundation of any long-lasting effect is the trust and respect that new leaders must earn from their team. To establish trustworthiness:

- Prior to making significant changes, it is important to respect the opinions of the current team by listening and observing.

- To minimize ambiguity, communicate transparently about goals, priorities, and any anticipated initial changes.

- In order to gain trust over time, it is important to keep your word.

Creating Initial Momentum: Although it's crucial to avoid placing too much emphasis on immediate results, early successes that are modest but noticeable can boost a leader's confidence. One way to create momentum is by:

- Recognizing and resolving low-hanging fruit problems or difficulties that are easily fixed.

- Celebrating little victories with the team shows the leader's dedication to team achievement and boosts morale.

- A clear vision and first roadmap that is in line with the objectives of the organization should be established.

Defining a Clear Vision: Early in their leadership career, leaders who convey a compelling vision aid their team in understanding the direction and goal of their work. An inspiring vision

- **Inspires the group** by giving them direction and a feeling of purpose.

- **Promotes alignment** on shared objectives, clearing up misunderstandings and boosting productivity.

- It facilitates the implementation of future projects by laying the groundwork for long-term strategies.

Creating an Open Line of Communication: Since they promote trust and lessen uncertainty, transparency and open communication are crucial throughout changes. Leaders ought to:

- Provide the team with regular updates on any new developments or strategy adjustments.

- In order to create an environment where team members feel appreciated and participated, it is important to promote feedback and communication.

- To address specific concerns and establish rapport,

schedule frequent check-ins and one-on-ones with team members.

Leaders must comprehend the opportunities and vulnerabilities present throughout transitions in order to navigate them successfully. Leaders may create a foundation that promotes trust, stimulates innovation, and is in line with long-term organizational objectives by steering clear of frequent errors, placing a high priority on relationship-building, and approaching the first ninety days strategically.

CHAPTER 2

GET READY BEFORE YOU BEGIN

Effective leadership transitions depend on preparation because it lays the foundation for comprehending the corporate environment, establishing important connections, and determining a practical course of action. Prior to taking any strategic action, executives need to understand the particular environment of the business, identify key players, and set reasonable goals that complement both short- and long-term objectives. This chapter thoroughly examines these fundamental actions, offering a framework that enables leaders to start their new positions with a strong foundation.

2.1 Evaluating Your Circumstance

Preparing for a successful leadership transition requires a thorough evaluation of oneself and the business. Leaders must assess the cultural dynamics, strengths, and weaknesses of the new organization. They should evaluate themselves at the same time to make sure that their leadership style, values, and skill set match those of the company.

Comprehending the Organization's Advantages and Disadvantages:

Leaders need to be able to swiftly identify the organization's strengths and weaknesses. This calls for:
- Examining current workflows and results to find any bottlenecks and effective procedures.
- Examining performance metrics to determine the organization's strong points and opportunities for development.
- Interviewing team members one-on-one to learn more about their cultural dynamics, daily struggles, and team morale.

Evaluating the Organizational Culture Every firm has a distinct culture that affects employee relationships, communication styles, and decision-making. Leaders ought to:

- Evaluate the organization's degree of formality, cooperation, and inclusivity by observing daily interactions.
- Determine the fundamental principles and unwritten rules that influence conduct. This could include preferences for innovation or tradition, the degree of risk tolerance, and the way conflicts are resolved.
- To validate and improve these findings, which can inform future choices, have an open discussion with team members and stakeholders.

Self-Evaluation and Alignment: Self-evaluation is equally as vital as comprehending the context of the organization. Leaders must assess their own values, talents, and shortcomings and think about how these fit with the culture of the company.

- A leader with good organizational abilities can be a great asset if the organization lacks a formal procedure but excels in creativity. This is an example of how to identify strengths that complement organizational shortcomings.
- In order to adjust to the new environment, it can be crucial to recognize one's own limitations and places

for improvement.
- In order to maintain motivation and integrity in leadership, it is imperative that personal values and goals are in line with the organization's mission.

2.2 Finding Important Stakeholders

The people or organizations that have sway, contribute resources, and affect decision-making are known as key stakeholders. To successfully navigate organizational dynamics and make sure that leaders get the support they need for their efforts, it is crucial to identify and cultivate connections with key stakeholders.

Comprehending the Influence Landscape: Stakeholders can include long-term staff members, unofficial team leaders, and those with specific knowledge in addition to those in official leadership positions. To find out who has power, knowledge, and respect in the company, leaders should:

- Map out official and informal networks.
- Find possible advocates and allies who can support and communicate new initiatives.
- Identify critics or skeptics who might oppose

change, as knowing their viewpoints at an early stage can help prevent disputes or miscommunications.

Interacting with Key Stakeholders: Developing relationships with stakeholders is about more than just acquiring power; it's about creating sincere bonds that can promote cooperation and trust. Successful leaders:

- Set up one-on-one sessions with important stakeholders to learn about their objectives, worries, and expectations.
- To get a thorough grasp of each stakeholder's values within the company and their opinions on the opportunities and difficulties that are currently facing it, it is important to ask open-ended questions.
- In order to foster goodwill and create opportunities for cooperation, it is important to show real interest in stakeholder perspectives and respect for their knowledge and ideas.

Simplifying Decision-Making With Stakeholder Assistance: Decision-making is simplified when stakeholders are involved because powerful people can hasten organizational buy-in. Strong relationships allow leaders to:

- Get early support for strategic initiatives, which increases the chances that they will be implemented successfully.
- Create a network of advisors who can offer advice and insights when new problems come up.
- By lowering resistance and promoting unity, leaders can get traction with more extensive organizational reforms by forming a coalition.

2.3 Establishing Reasonable Goals

To avoid burnout, make significant progress, and create the foundation for long-term success, it is crucial to set clear and reasonable expectations for the first few months. Leaders must adopt a well-rounded strategy that incorporates determining viability, establishing quantifiable goals, and coordinating with organizational priorities.

Knowing What's Feasible: Leaders should steer clear of the pitfalls of trying to do too much too quickly, as this can result in disappointment and fatigue for both the team and

the leader. To establish realistic objectives:
- To determine the extent of what can be achieved in a realistic manner, it is necessary to evaluate the availability of resources, including time, money, and talent.
- Take into account the organization's rate of change; some are more quick to adjust to new projects, while others take longer.
- Make sure the leader's first efforts support the organization's larger goals by setting priorities that are in line with both short-term demands and long-term ambitions.

Setting Actionable and Measurable Goals: In order to make progress visible and allow for required modifications, leaders must convert expectations into concrete actions that can be monitored and measured.
- **Specify short-term objectives** that can show early success and generate momentum. These could be quick wins that boost team morale and productivity, team-building activities, or process enhancements.
- To create a sense of accomplishment and advancement, it is important to divide major goals

into smaller, more achievable tasks with distinct due dates and roles.
- For every goal, set quantifiable outcomes (KPIs or metrics) that allow leaders to monitor their influence and offer concrete proof of success.

Aligning Goals with Stakeholder Expectations: Leaders should establish expectations that are in line with their stakeholders' interests and that are also reasonable. This guarantees that their work is useful and appreciated by the company.
- To ensure alignment and get support for early goals, it is important to have an open discussion about expectations with key stakeholders.
- Modify objectives if required in response to input, ensuring that initial efforts align with the organization's aims and values.
- Communicate progress to stakeholders on a regular basis, including updates on long-term projects and acknowledging minor victories to foster openness and confidence.

Leaders must carefully evaluate the organizational

environment, locate and interact with key stakeholders, and establish reasonable goals for the first few years of their position in order to prepare for a smooth transition. Leaders can build a solid foundation for good impact by tackling these phases with a planned and deliberate mentality. This will help them overcome obstacles and take advantage of opportunities as they guide the organization forward.

CHAPTER 3

Getting Results Early

For new leaders, achieving early victories is essential because it builds credibility, garners team support, and sets a favorable tone for subsequent projects. Early victories provide momentum that can assist overcome resistance and foster trust, and they show that a leader can make significant changes, even in a short amount of time. This chapter examines the importance of early victories, how to pinpoint the best locations for them, and how to put changes into place that produce results immediately.

3.1 The Importance of Early Victories

Early victories are crucial in determining how people view a leader's skills and style since they offer verifiable proof of their dedication and efficacy. By demonstrating that the leader is committed to implementing constructive changes, these brief successes are crucial for boosting confidence both inside the team and throughout the larger business.

Building Credibility and Trust One of the most pressing issues facing leaders is establishing credibility. Quick wins can:

- Exhibit capability and decisiveness, giving stakeholders and team members confidence that the leader is capable and proactive.
- It's important to make a good first impression since first impressions tend to stick with you. Establishing confidence early on is facilitated by demonstrating the ability to produce results.
- As team members frequently want evidence that the leader's vision is in line with their requirements and that they will be assisted in accomplishing common objectives, it is important to build trust via action.

The team's morale can be boosted by early victories, which demonstrate that development is achievable and that the leader appreciates everyone's contributions.

- Encourage enthusiasm and dedication to impending changes by instilling faith in the new leader's strategy and vision.

- Showing that the team leader cares about their achievement and well-being will increase team engagement. A leader who proactively works to produce outcomes early on instills a sense of accountability in the group.
- Encourage open communication since team members are more willing to share ideas and criticism when they feel their efforts will be appreciated.

Building Momentum for Future ventures: By creating a sense of excitement and energy that carries over into more complicated tasks, early victories lay the groundwork for future ventures.
- By demonstrating to the group that success is attainable and that upcoming projects will be handled with the same commitment and effectiveness, you may set a favorable precedent.
- Create a domino effect in which little successes increase trust in the leader's strategic vision, which facilitates securing support for more difficult projects.
- As early achievements highlight the effectiveness of

the leader's strategy and foster a more transformation-friendly atmosphere, they can help reduce resistance to change.

3.2 Determining Early Success Areas

Since these early victories must be noticeable and significant, choosing the best areas for them calls for strategic thinking. Leaders may show that they can swiftly add value while meeting important organizational needs by concentrating on areas where changes can yield a strong return on investment.

Focusing on High-Visibility Issues: By tackling issues that are well recognized and highly visible, a leader may make sure that a large audience notices their efforts.
- Because fixing these problems would be highly appreciated by team members and stakeholders, choose initiatives that address frequent frustrations or inefficiencies.
- Initiatives involving cross-functional collaboration should be taken into consideration, as their accomplishments can show a leader's capacity to

collaborate across departments and promote teamwork.

- **Use data and feedback** to identify places that are known to cause pain for consumers or staff, as doing so will have a positive and noticeable effect.

Selecting Projects with Immediate Impact: Leaders should give priority to projects that can be finished quickly but yield significant outcomes, establishing a direct connection between the new leadership and constructive change.

- Projects or concerns that have been neglected or put off because of a lack of funding or guidance are known as "low-hanging fruit."
- Pay attention to process enhancements, since little changes to procedures can result in instant productivity increases that the team can readily observe and value.
- By making minor changes that increase customer pleasure, such as expedited service, quicker response times, or better communication, you can improve customer experience.

- Balancing Complexity with Speed Early victories must be attainable in a short amount of time, but they must also be significant enough to show leadership potential.
- Aim for projects that can be finished in a few weeks or months, avoiding complicated problems that can take longer.
- Make sure that the early victories are not isolated triumphs but rather contribute to larger strategic goals by choosing adjustments that are in line with long-term aims.
- To ensure that early successes do not exhaust resources required for later, more extensive projects, it is important to be aware of resource limitations.

3.3 Putting Early Changes into Practice

Action, communication, and follow-through must be carefully balanced for early victories to be implemented successfully. In addition to implementing changes, leaders must make sure they are carried out successfully and are accepted by the organization.

Creating a Clear Action Plan: Leaders require a methodical strategy with well-defined objectives, deadlines, and resources in order to attain early victories.

- Make sure everyone on the team is aware of their part in the project by clearly outlining their roles and responsibilities.
- Define precise success metrics so that outcomes are visible and progress is quantifiable. Time savings, customer satisfaction ratings, or decreased error rates are a few examples of metrics.
- To keep the project from getting behind schedule and losing steam, develop a realistic timeline that accounts for any probable obstacles.

Effective communication is essential to making sure that changes are understood and welcomed by the organization.

- Explain each change's purpose to the team and stakeholders, highlighting how it supports the group's overall objectives and fits in with organizational goals.
- Ask for input at every stage, which makes team members feel engaged and can yield insightful information that enhances execution.

- To acknowledge the team's efforts and promote a culture of advancement and success, it is important to celebrate minor triumphs along the way.

Exhibiting Leadership and Vision: Leaders should use early victories to highlight their principles, leadership style, and organizational vision.

- **Set an example** by exhibiting dedication, openness, and fortitude when implementing changes and overcoming obstacles.
- Exhibit flexibility by being willing to make changes in response to team input or changing conditions.
- In order to help team members comprehend the objective of each effort and promote alignment with long-term goals, it is important to highlight the influence of early wins on the larger organizational mission.

Building the Foundation for Future Projects: Early victories should not be isolated triumphs, but rather should pave the way for later, more noteworthy accomplishments.

- Early successes might be used as a springboard to garner support for larger, more ambitious ventures.

The crew is more inclined to support bigger projects when they witness positive results.

- In order to reinforce excellent practices and steer clear of potential dangers, it is important to document triumphs and lessons gained so that early victories can be used as case studies for subsequent projects.
- Create a culture of continuous improvement by motivating team members to look for chances for future successes and offer suggestions that support the strategic vision of the leader.

Leaders must use early wins as a key tactic to increase trust, garner support, and create momentum for longer-term projects. Leaders may guarantee a seamless and successful transition into their new role by concentrating on high-visibility, high-impact areas, making changes with clear communication and organized action plans, and building on these successes to achieve future success. These early successes not only show proficiency and dedication, but they also promote a culture of cooperation, advancement, and success for everybody.

CHAPTER 4

ACQUIRING KNOWLEDGE OF THE TERRAIN

Any leadership change must include learning the local environment. A new leader needs to comprehend the organization's processes, culture, networks, and team dynamics in order to lead effectively. In order to promote well-informed decision-making and lay the groundwork for enduring partnerships, this chapter explores the essential components of carrying out in-depth organizational research, mapping internal networks, and assessing team dynamics.

4.1 Performing Research in Organizations

An essential first step in leadership transitions is organizational research, which gives leaders knowledge about the team's established procedures, objectives, and difficulties. By doing this study strategically and thoroughly, leaders can steer clear of pitfalls and develop well-informed plans.

Comprehending the Structure and Procedures of Organizations: Finding possible areas for improvement requires a thorough understanding of the organization's operations.

- To comprehend current operating standards, carefully examine recorded procedures and workflows, paying particular attention to any areas designated for recent modifications or ongoing improvement.
- Find inefficiencies and bottlenecks by examining procedures that impact output or team spirit. When proposing or putting improvements into practice, this understanding will be helpful.
- The organization's main decision-making processes should be mapped out, including who usually makes choices, how they are made, and where approvals are needed. This realization aids a leader in implementing changes while adhering to established procedures.

Gathering Insights from Stakeholder Interviews: One of

the best methods for getting first hand information from those who have a deep understanding of the company is conducting stakeholder interviews.

- To find out about the expectations, priorities, and concerns of each stakeholder, prepare strategic questions. "What do you see as the biggest opportunity for improvement in our processes?" is one example.
- "What issues do you think need our attention the most right now?"
- Throughout these conversations, pay attention to any recurring themes or concerns. Recurring issues are high priority for first attempts since they frequently indicate fundamental issues inside the company.
- By demonstrating to stakeholders that you appreciate their opinions and are dedicated to understanding the organization from their points of view, you may build rapport and trust through open communication.

In order to align with the organization's principles and steer clear of pitfalls, it is imperative to observe organizational culture.

- Keep an eye on how teams interact and

communicate, observing whether the culture values formal gatherings or casual conversations. You can adjust your communication style with the use of this.

- Keep an eye out for outward manifestations of the company's principles, like mission statements, branding collateral, and charitable endeavors. It will be easier to match organizational principles with your leadership style if you are aware of the cultural foundations.

- Identify taboos and unwritten norms that influence team dynamics and day-to-day operations. For instance, whereas some organizations promote individual initiative and quick decision-making, others favor decisions that are made by agreement.

4.2 Internal Network Mapping

Formal and informal internal networks have an impact on decision-making processes, information flow, and teamwork. Leaders who comprehend these networks are better able to negotiate power dynamics and make use of communication channels.

Determining Important Gatekeepers and Influencers: Informal leaders frequently have a big impact on team morale and project momentum; official titles alone don't always reflect influence.

- Determine which individuals, whether by tenure, experience, or personal connections, have a great deal of influence inside their teams. These influencers can be very helpful allies in securing support and advancing projects.
- Identify gatekeepers who manage access to resources, information, or authorizations. Project progress can be facilitated and bureaucratic delays avoided by knowing how to collaborate with these people.
- Influence should be taken into account at all organizational levels, from CEOs to team leads and seasoned team members who are familiar with the company's history and unspoken standards.

Comprehending Informal Communication Channels: Informal networks can provide insights not easily available through formal channels and frequently speed up the transmission of information.

- **Watch how teams** share knowledge, whether it's through regular meetings, online forums, or informal face-to-face encounters. This can provide knowledge on how to efficiently disseminate information.
- Find ways to influence people outside of the organizational hierarchy, including mentorship connections, regular lunch groups, or group chats. The fundamental factors that influence how work is done can be uncovered by these unofficial networks.
- Make use of these networks to obtain candid input on ongoing projects or initiatives. Concerns that would not come out in professional contexts can frequently be revealed in casual talks.

Building Relationships inside the Network: The quality of relationships with important members is a vital factor in navigating internal networks effectively.

- Take the time to establish rapport with individuals from all levels and roles, demonstrating respect for their expertise.
- To establish trust and show that you genuinely care about the team's requirements, have casual conversations outside of scheduled meetings.

- By expressing gratitude for contributions and recognizing the unofficial network leaders, you can build goodwill and increase their willingness to assist you.

4.3 Team Dynamics Analysis

Every team has distinct dynamics that are influenced by past collaborations, interpersonal ties, and individual strengths. Leaders can spot potential disputes, areas of strength, and places where team members might need more support by having a quick knowledge of these interactions.

Identifying Team Strengths and Weaknesses: Leaders may more effectively match positions with capabilities when they are aware of the abilities and limitations of their team members.
- **Conduct skills assessments** to determine the team's capabilities. This can be more formal, like performance reviews, or more informal, like going over previous projects.
- To improve teamwork, combine people with various strengths to find complementary skill sets that can

promote collaboration.

- Make a note of any capability gaps that could compromise the project's success. Leaders can prioritize hiring, training, or reassigning resources as needed when these are identified early.

Interpersonal Relationships and Tensions: Understanding Interpersonal interactions have an impact on team productivity, and unresolved conflicts can impede advancement.

- By observing who collaborates successfully with others and where disagreements occur, you can observe patterns of collaboration and tension. This can offer valuable perspectives on how to allocate tasks and handle possible disputes.
- Promote an atmosphere where team members feel free to voice their issues and offer feedback to one another by encouraging open communication. The establishment of safe spaces for discussion can frequently aid in the resolution of conflicts.
- Within the team, look for groups and alliances. Although strong alliances can improve teamwork, if factions are not handled properly, they can divert a

team's attention and undermine cohesiveness.

Evaluating Team Engagement and Morale: A driven team is more innovative and productive. To determine which sectors require a morale boost, leaders should assess morale.

- Measure team satisfaction and excitement using surveys, group gatherings, or one-on-one discussions. Team members' opinions on the opportunities and difficulties of the present should be actively heard by leaders.
- Determine the causes of low morale, such as burnout, a lack of recognition, or ambiguous goals, and devise plans to deal with them. Simple actions like praising accomplishments or outlining expectations may frequently make a big difference right away.
- Encourage an environment of openness and trust because a team that feels informed and trusted is more likely to stay motivated and involved.

Supporting the Team's Growth and growth: Team growth should be a continuous priority for leaders, who should match their own aspirations with those of the company.

- Promote professional development and skill-building by offering chances for mentorship, training, or difficult assignments. In addition to enhancing capabilities, this demonstrates to team members the leader's commitment to their future.
- Assist people and groups in establishing goals, making sure that each member has specific, attainable objectives that support the success of the company as a whole.
- To promote a culture of ongoing development, mentor and coach team members. Team members can develop their confidence and skill sets by participating in cross-functional collaboration opportunities, career conversations, and regular feedback sessions.

Studying the lay of the land necessitates a purposeful, methodical approach to comprehending the internal workings of the business, the networks that influence it, and the team dynamics that propel day-to-day activities. A strong basis for well-informed decision-making and fruitful, constructive interactions can be established by leaders through organizational research, internal network mapping, and team dynamics analysis. With this understanding, leaders may make significant changes that meet both short-term demands and long-term goals while also adjusting to the company culture.

CHAPTER 5

Getting Important Stakeholders to Support You Early

One of the most important things a leader can do when taking on a new role is to get support from important stakeholders. In addition to bringing stakeholders together around shared objectives, early buy-in lays the groundwork for future success by fostering mutual respect and trust. Leaders may create positive momentum and facilitate decision-making, cooperation, and project support by proactively building good connections with peers, superiors, and direct subordinates. The key elements of successfully establishing these connections are covered in this chapter.

5.1 Establishing Connections with Superiors

Building solid, open relationships with higher management is crucial for new leaders. A positive working connection with superiors guarantees goal congruence and makes expectations clear, fostering an environment that supports a leader's success.

Creating Open Channels of contact: Leaders should set the example for open, frequent, and honest contact with superiors.

- Early on, set up frequent one-on-one meetings to go over goals, talk about obstacles, and get input. Check-ins every week or every two weeks can help to maintain goal alignment and quickly address any new issues.
- Establish preferred communication channels and times. While some leaders might welcome informal updates, others would prefer in-depth reports. Making these preferences clear guarantees that the superior is always aware and helps prevent misunderstandings.
- To establish trust and demonstrate to superiors that progress is being achieved, share early victories and brief updates. To show immediate influence, emphasize quantifiable results.

To ensure that efforts are in line with organizational priorities, it is imperative to have a clear understanding of expectations and goals.

- To determine the main aims and objectives for the first several months, ask targeted questions. Questions such as "What are your top priorities for our team over the next quarter?" may be part of this.
- "What important metrics or results should we prioritize?"
- To demonstrate proactive alignment, align early endeavors with your superior's aims and identify places where quick wins can help their objectives.
- Together with your supervisor, establish clear performance indicators and benchmarks. Both parties can monitor progress and make necessary modifications thanks to this.

Cultivating Transparency and Trust Transparency, openness, and dependability are necessary to establish trust with superiors.

- Exhibit dependability by fulfilling early commitments and completing projects on time. Your dependability and commitment to achieving

common objectives must be evident to superiors.
- Potential difficulties should be openly discussed, along with your plan of action. When problems are openly discussed and solutions are provided, confidence is increased and credibility is increased.
- To demonstrate your dedication to ongoing development and alignment with your superior's vision, you should ask for honest feedback and show that you are receptive to criticism.

5.2 Building Trust with Colleagues

Peers are crucial to a leader's capacity to carry out tasks and accomplish objectives in any kind of company. Working together with peers guarantees that leaders may take advantage of common resources, knowledge, and assistance, which frequently make or break projects. Building respect and trust with peers early on and consistently can have a long-lasting favorable effect on achievement in general.

Building Open, Collaborative Relationships: Respect and proactive involvement are necessary to cultivate a cooperative environment with peers.

- Arrange for initial meetings with colleagues from various departments or roles. Learn about each person's duties, ongoing initiatives, and objectives during these discussions.
- Demonstrate a sincere interest in their job and difficulties, providing support when necessary. This promotes a cooperative environment and aids in laying the groundwork for respect for one another.
- Explain your own experience, qualifications, and goals, emphasizing areas where cooperation would be useful. By sharing information about your interests and areas of experience, peers are more likely to view you as a resource.

Identifying Shared Objectives and Opportunities for Cooperation: Leaders who are able to coordinate their projects with those of their colleagues establish a feeling of unity.

- Find areas where the goals of your peers and your projects overlap. Collaboration can result in shared successes and efficiencies when objectives are in line.

- When appropriate, form cross-functional working groups to provide colleagues a chance to participate in and gain from your projects.
- Make strategic use of shared resources. For instance, if the resources or knowledge needed for your project and a peer's project are similar, think about combining them for increased efficiency.

Preserving Diplomacy and Respect: Disagreements about priorities or viewpoints can occur even in a cooperative setting. Maintaining long-term, fruitful relationships requires handling these circumstances diplomatically.

- Recognize that every department has its own goals and obstacles, and respect the boundaries and priorities of other teams.
- Approach disagreements with a problem-solving mentality, putting the shared objectives ahead of individual viewpoints. This guarantees that conversations stay positive and focused on finding solutions.
- Acknowledge the contributions of colleagues by celebrating joint accomplishments. Recognition by

the public promotes goodwill and future collaboration.

5.3 Winning Direct Reports' Trust

Building trust with direct reports is the first step in creating a cohesive, driven, and cooperative team. To gain respect, encourage participation, and establish a supportive atmosphere where team members feel appreciated and encouraged to contribute, new leaders must put in a lot of effort.

Building Credibility Right Away: Direct subordinates look to their boss for confidence in judgments, direction, and advice. Establishing credibility early on aids in strengthening their dedication and trust.

- Help the team understand how their job fits into the larger company goals by properly communicating your vision and goals.
- Explain your experience and expertise, particularly if your background fits well with the projects or objectives your team is working on right now. Being knowledgeable and competent gives the team

confidence that they are in good hands.
- It demonstrates your dedication to comprehending the team dynamic and leveraging it to improve productivity when you take the time to learn about each team member's contributions and skills.

Establishing a Foundation of Openness and Mutual Respect:

- Direct reporting must feel heard and valued. A collaborative, productive team is fostered by leaders that promote transparency.
- In order to demonstrate that you value team members' perspectives and are prepared to make adjustments when necessary, you should actively listen to them and appreciate their comments.
- Establish a setting where team members can freely voice their worries or recommendations. A stronger team culture and increased levels of engagement result when members of the team feel free to be honest.
- Set a good example by communicating in a courteous manner. Make sure team members feel encouraged rather than chastised by carefully

considering feedback and constructive criticism.

Promoting Ownership and Engagement: A motivated team is an engaged team. Direct reports feel more invested in the group's success when their leaders encourage ownership and participation.

- Each team member should be given significant responsibilities so they may accept responsibility for their work. Giving team members significant responsibilities shows that you have faith in their skills.
- When appropriate, include team members in decision-making procedures. Allowing direct reports to participate in some decision-making processes promotes agency and demonstrates that their opinions are respected.
- To boost a sense of accomplishment and motivate ongoing work, it is important to celebrate victories and milestones, both team-wide and individual.

In order to assist team members feel safe and focused, new leaders should offer the support and direction they need on a regular basis.

- Be accessible for inquiries and guidance, particularly in the early stages of a project. Your assistance and presence foster trust and provide the team with self-assurance in carrying out their duties.
- Regularly and constructively provide constructive criticism, highlighting strengths and offering practical suggestions for development. A leader who gives helpful, unambiguous instructions has a higher chance of earning the trust of direct reports.
- Through mentoring, training, or exposure to new initiatives, provide opportunities for learning and development. Leaders show their dedication to the team's long-term success by making investments in their professional growth.

Building solid, open, and encouraging relationships with peers, superiors, and direct reports is the first step in gaining support from important stakeholders. Leaders that take the effort to establish trust, make expectations clear, and promote teamwork create a favorable atmosphere that can continue to develop momentum for subsequent projects. Leaders may create an atmosphere where everyone feels appreciated, in sync, and inspired to work together to achieve common objectives by carefully cultivating relationships.

CHAPTER 6

MATCHING ORGANIZATIONAL OBJECTIVES WITH VISION

More than simply managerial abilities are needed for effective leadership; the team must be united and motivated by a compelling vision. A cohesive, driven, and productive team is produced when a leader's vision and the objectives of the organization are in line. Since it establishes a foundation of trust, clarity, and shared purpose, this alignment is particularly important in the early stages of leadership. This chapter describes how to create a personal leadership vision that aligns with organizational goals and personal values, set short- and long-term objectives that strike a balance between sustainable growth and quick wins, and communicate this vision so that all team members are aware of and motivated by the leader's guidance.

6.1 Outlining a Vision for Personal Leadership

Since it establishes the tone for their approach, priorities, and values, developing a personal leadership vision is an essential first step for new leaders. This vision should act as a compass, directing choices and motivating the group to accomplish short-term and long-term objectives.

Aligning Personal Values with Organizational Goals: A clear leadership vision integrates personal values with the organization's mission and goals.

- Consider your own ideals and motivations. Questions like "What drives me as a leader?" and "What impact do I want to make?" are important for leaders to ask themselves. Leaders may develop an authentic vision by determining the fundamental motives and values.
- Comprehend the mission and strategic objectives of the organization. To grasp the organization's goals, leaders should review its mission statement, strategic priorities, and recent achievements.
- Determine the points of alignment. Identify the precise areas where organizational objectives and personal values coincide. A CEO who appreciates innovation, for example, would concentrate on

leading initiatives that strengthen the company's competitive edge.

Setting a Clear and Inspiring Direction: A successful vision is both realistic and aspirational, giving team members a clear path forward and motivating them to work toward a greater goal.

- Explain the long-term goal and intended effect. Leaders should outline their goals for the group or organization they are leading, emphasizing both measurable and intangible results.
- Make sure it's relevant and feasible. Confusion or annoyance might result from a vision that is too ambitious or unrelated to the organization's primary goal. Realism and inspiration should be balanced.
- It is important to include flexibility. The vision should be adaptable enough to change while upholding the organization's basic principles and goals as market conditions or organizational priorities change.

6.2 Establishing Both Short- and Long-Term Objectives

The next stage after establishing the leadership vision is to convert it into attainable objectives. In order to generate momentum, leaders must both short-term and long-term objectives. These objectives must be reasonable, quantifiable, and in line with the organization's overarching plan.

Balancing Immediate Impact with Future Growth: To establish credibility and lay the groundwork for long-term success, leaders should set goals that yield immediate results.

- Finding "quick wins" that support the vision is the first step. Early on, concentrate on attainable goals that show the worth of the leader's vision. These could be minor enhancements to customer happiness, staff morale, or process efficiency.
- Create long-term objectives that promote long-term success. Although they can take time to accomplish, objectives like developing new products, expanding the market, or training employees offer long-term benefits. To track progress and maintain team engagement, set milestones for these objectives.
- Take into account the availability of resources.

Assess the team's capabilities, financial constraints, and available resources to establish challenging yet attainable objectives. While attainable goals foster confidence, overly optimistic ones can result in exhaustion.

Setting SMART objectives: SMART stands for specified, measurable, achievable, relevant, and time-bound goals.

- **Specific:** Clearly state the tasks that must be completed. Use the phrase "increase team productivity by 15% in six months" rather than "improve team performance."
- **Measurable:** Use metrics to quantify progress. For example, "finish five new client projects by Q4" is a precise, quantifiable goal.
- **Achievable:** Establish reasonable goals in light of present capabilities and available resources. The squad may become demotivated by unrealistic goals.
- Make sure the objective is in line with the organization's mission and the leader's vision. Every objective ought to make a significant contribution to more general strategic aims.
- **Time-bound:** Establish due dates to foster

accountability and urgency. While lengthier timescales for complicated tasks offer a defined path, shorter timelines for immediate goals can create momentum.

In order to monitor progress and guarantee conformity with the vision, goals should be accompanied by accountability measures.

- Assign responsibility for every objective. Assigning tasks to particular team members or departments promotes accountability and gives the group the chance to take charge.
- Perform progress reviews and check-ins on a regular basis. Hold quarterly or monthly meetings to discuss issues, evaluate progress, and make necessary corrections.
- Reward achievements. Acknowledging accomplishments, no matter how minor, strengthens dedication to objectives and inspires the group to keep moving forward.

6.3 Expressing the Goal

A vision that is not shared is a lost chance. Leaders must efficiently and concisely convey their vision to the team in order to promote comprehension, zeal, and unity. Team members are more likely to devote themselves entirely to realizing the goal when they comprehend and share it.

Creating an Engaging Story: Leaders should explain their vision in a way that emotionally engaged team members in order to gain buy-in.

- Let's start with the "why." Describe the vision's purpose, the significance of the objectives, and the ways in which they will benefit the team and the organization. To foster a sense of community and encourage internal drive, highlight common ideals.
- Emphasize the path and destination. Explain the team's current situation, the future course, and the advantages of realizing the goal. A leader might state, for instance, "We want to be known as the most creative and customer-focused team in our industry in three years."
- Include instances from actual life. The vision becomes more relatable and pertinent when it is connected to current issues, industry trends, or

customer demands.

Using Multiple Communication Channels: Team members can more easily internalize and maintain alignment with the vision when it is reinforced via repetition and a variety of communication techniques.

- Present the vision during a team or all-hands meeting. This offers a chance for preliminary conversation and real-time resolution of any queries or issues.
- Make use of written formats. After the meeting, send a written paper or email outlining the expectations, goals, and vision. This formalizes the message and acts as a point of reference.
- Make use of unofficial means of communication. In daily contacts, consistently reaffirm the vision. The team's mindset can be ingrained with the vision through quick reminders, informal check-ins, and casual interactions.

Promoting Feedback and Dialogue: Feedback loops and open talks foster an inclusive environment and show the leader's dedication to a team-based vision.

- Encourage team members to discuss their thoughts and ask questions. Feedback-friendly leaders encourage team members to take ownership of the project, which strengthens dedication to the goal.
- Individual concerns should be addressed in one-on-one sessions. Members of the team could have particular queries or worries that they would rather talk about in private. These meetings offer a chance to address any reservations and clear up any misunderstandings.
- Constructive criticism should be acknowledged and taken into consideration. When possible, include team recommendations into the vision or associated objectives. This demonstrates that the vision is a team effort rather than an order.

Building Shared Ownership of the Vision: Team members are more likely to be dedicated to the success of the vision when they believe they have a share in it.

- Team members should be encouraged to take the initiative. Assign tasks or initiatives that enable people to actively participate in the realization of the vision. A team member might, for instance, take the lead on a project that fits with a certain short-term objective.

- Acknowledge contributions that advance the vision. Recognizing initiatives that support the vision in public encourages others to get involved.
- Together, commemorate significant occasions. Collaboratively recognize and honor successes, highlighting how each one advances the group toward realizing the common goal.

Establishing a personal leadership vision, establishing inspirational and attainable goals, and skillfully conveying this vision to the team are all necessary steps in ensuring alignment between vision and corporate goals. Effective leaders encourage their teams to work passionately and resolutely toward common objectives by striking a balance between immediate successes and long-term ambitions. Leaders create the conditions for a cohesive, driven team that is prepared to take on challenges and produce exceptional results by encouraging a culture of openness, cooperation, and shared ownership.

CHAPTER 7

EVALUATING AND DEVELOPING YOUR GROUP

One of the most important elements of effective leadership is the leader's capacity to create and nurture a high-achieving team. Understanding team members' present ability levels, spotting talent gaps, and strategically choosing who to hire or reorganize can lay the groundwork for both immediate and long-term success. This chapter describes the crucial procedures for evaluating a team's advantages and disadvantages, creating individualized growth plans for team members, and making important hiring decisions that support the objectives of the team and the company.

7.1 Assessing the Strengths and Weaknesses of the Team

Understanding the existing status of the team is the first step towards creating an effective one. The team's abilities, experiences, and competencies must be thoroughly evaluated by leaders in order to identify areas that require help or development as well as strengths that can be capitalized on.

Performing a Team Skills Audit: A skills audit gives an overview of the team's present competencies.

- Examine current job duties and obligations. Assess whether the roles of team members are in line with their areas of strength. Productivity might be hampered when roles and skills are not aligned.
- Evaluate both soft and technical talents. Communication, problem-solving, and collaborative abilities are just as important as technical competencies. A balanced skill set is necessary for a well-rounded team.
- Determine your areas of competence and specialized knowledge. Determine whether team members possess specialized expertise that can be used for special projects or objectives.
- Assess learning agility and adaptability. The capacity to learn and adapt is essential in fields that are undergoing rapid change. Find team members that

are willing to learn new abilities and who are at ease with change.

The utilization of assessment tools and feedback mechanisms can offer an objective perspective on the team's capabilities.

- 360-degree feedback is provided. To obtain a comprehensive understanding of each team member's performance, gather opinions from peers, coworkers, and subordinates.
- Performance evaluations. Evaluate prior performance and opportunities for development to determine whether more training or reorganization is required.
- Tools for self-evaluation. Team members should be encouraged to evaluate their own abilities and potential development areas. This promotes self-awareness and aids in locating possible areas for growth.

The process of mapping out areas for improvement and skills gaps: After identifying the team's strengths, it's critical to identify any gaps that can affect its performance.

- The first step is to identify any mission-critical skill deficiencies. Give top priority on the abilities that are necessary to achieve short-term goals. For instance, make sure the team is sufficiently skilled in data analysis if it is a crucial part of future projects.
- Take into account future requirements. As the team takes on additional tasks or the company expands, anticipate the talents that may be needed. Developing these abilities proactively can ultimately save time and money.
- Recognize the differences between team and individual gaps. Sometimes educating one team member rather than employing a new one is a better way to close a talent gap. In other situations, establishing a new position or enlisting outside assistance can be the best way to close the gap.

7.2 Formulating Team Member Development Plans

The foundation of a good team is ongoing development and education. Individualized development strategies boost engagement, boost morale, and help close skill gaps. Development plans must be clear, attainable, and in line with the demands of the company as well as the goals of the individual.

Establishing Specific Development Goals: To begin, specify what each team member's development plan is intended to accomplish.

- Goals should be in line with corporate objectives. Make sure the learning process is relevant and purpose-driven by connecting the development plan to the organization's overarching objectives.
- Both short-term and long-term objectives should be included. While long-term goals could include advanced technical training or leadership, short-term aims can concentrate on immediate skill development.
- Adapt objectives to personal desires. Supporting employees' own aspirations increases their motivation. For example, think about including leadership training if a team member wants to advance into management.

Effective development demands more than just goal-setting; it also requires the proper resources and continuous leadership support.

- Education and training. Make workshops, classes, certifications, or lectures accessible. Depending on the skill being cultivated, these may be internal or external.
- Coaching and mentoring. Assign team members to mentors who can offer direction, criticism, and support. In addition to enhancing abilities, mentoring boosts self-esteem.
- Opportunities for learning on the job. Motivate team members to embark on new tasks or initiatives that will enable them to use and hone their abilities. Experience in the real world is one of the best methods to learn.
- Loops of feedback. Team members are able to monitor their progress and modify their growth plans as needed through frequent check-ins and constructive feedback sessions.

The implementation of accountability measures is crucial for the effectiveness of development initiatives.

- Regular progress reviews are conducted. Set up meetings on a monthly or quarterly basis to review progress, resolve issues, and modify objectives as necessary.

- Establish quantifiable benchmarks. Development goals that are broken down into milestones provide for simpler management and visibility of progress. For example, a six-month course can be broken up into practical applications or monthly tasks.

- Promote introspection. Invite team members to evaluate their own development and provide feedback on their strengths and areas for improvement. Self-reflection increases responsibility and aids in the improvement of future development plans.

7.3 Selecting New Hires and Reassignments

Leaders may determine that changes to the team's composition are required after assessing the team's strengths and skill deficiencies. In order to meet urgent needs, this may entail moving team members to positions where they can be more productive or hiring new personnel. Effective personnel decisions can boost overall productivity, enhance team performance, and better match with business objectives.

Evaluating Reassignment Opportunities: Redistributing current team members to different positions or duties can improve team output.

- Find inconsistencies in existing roles. A team member in a tactical capacity who is exceptionally skilled at strategic thinking might be more appropriate for a more analytical or leadership-focused function.
- Take cross-functional talents into consideration. Certain team members might possess abilities that could help other departments inside the company. Reassignments can promote departmental cooperation and increase the team's knowledge base.
- Performance issues should be addressed. A reassignment to a more suitable role could boost morale and productivity if some team members are having trouble in their existing roles.

Assessing the Requirement for New Employees: Hiring new talent could be the best course of action when internal skill shortages cannot be filled. Strategic hiring facilitates the introduction of new viewpoints and specialized knowledge.

- Define the position and the necessary abilities. Clearly define the role's requirements and the particular abilities required before starting the hiring process. This guarantees a focused and effective hiring procedure.
- Strike a balance between cultural fit and skill. Employing people who share the team's beliefs and working style is crucial for cohesiveness, even when technical abilities are important. Cultural fit reduces the chance of turnover and fosters a healthy work atmosphere.
- Take into account both short-term and long-term requirements. Assess if the position is a short-term fix for an existing shortfall or if it will be required in the long run. It may be less expensive to hire a consultant or contractor for short-term requirements.

The successful integration of new hires necessitates meticulous preparation in order to guarantee a seamless transition and compatibility with team dynamics.

- The training and onboarding process. Introduce new

hires to the organization's culture, principles, and procedures through thorough onboarding. A well-organized training program speeds up their assimilation.

- Assign friends or mentors. Assign new hires to seasoned team members who can help them get settled in and navigate the early going.
- Make sure that expectations are clear. Communicate the new hire's duties, objectives, and role within the team from the very beginning. Having clear expectations reduces uncertainty and lays the groundwork for success.

Team building and assessment are dynamic, ongoing processes that call for a blend of strategic decision-making, individual growth planning, and objective evaluation. A resilient, flexible, and high-performing team is produced by leaders who take the time to identify the strengths and weaknesses of their group, make strategic hiring decisions, and engage in specialized growth opportunities. Teams that are built on a foundation of trust, competence, and unity are better able to handle the demands of the fast-paced business world of today and promote long-term organizational success.

CHAPTER 8

IMPLEMENTING EFFICIENT PROCEDURES

The effectiveness, morale, and success of a team can be significantly impacted by a leader's capacity to create or improve efficient procedures. In the early phases of their position, new leaders may guarantee a seamless, unified operational environment that supports both short-term and long-term goals by concentrating on fundamental operations. Leaders may establish a foundation for long-term productivity and foster an atmosphere where each team member's work is organized, purposeful, and in line with the objectives of the company by identifying critical operational procedures, optimizing workflows, and putting strategic changes into place.

8.1 Determining Important Operational Procedures

The first step in comprehending a team's basic functioning is identifying its major operational processes. During this phase, key workflows are mapped out, their efficacy is evaluated, and areas for improvement are identified.

Mapping Out Core Processes: Team leaders should gain a thorough grasp of the everyday tasks and fundamental duties of the group. This entails examining every phase of the process from beginning to end, identifying its purpose, and determining how it advances more general objectives. For instance:

- **Define major tasks and workflows:** Determine the tasks that are necessary for the team to accomplish its goals. Depending on the role of the team, this could involve data analysis, project planning, or customer interaction.

- **Separate each step of the process:** Examine every phase of important processes to comprehend the flow of events and how they support overarching goals. This analysis identifies areas that might use more resources or simplification, as well as bottlenecks and possible delays.

- **Determine process dependencies**: A team's work frequently requires input from other departments. Leaders can ensure more seamless cross-functional operations by prioritizing good communication and aligning schedules or resources when they are aware of these dependencies.

Interacting with Team Members: Leaders get a great deal from firsthand knowledge of the processes they plan to improve. Members of the team that work on daily operations frequently have firsthand knowledge of process problems or inefficiencies.

- **Have individual interviews or group conversations:** These discussions may reveal common bottlenecks, pain points, or suggestions for process enhancements. Inefficiencies that aren't readily apparent from the outside may be disclosed by team members.
- **Make use of feedback instruments such as surveys**: Team members can openly share ideas and offer candid feedback using anonymous surveys, especially when it comes to delicate topics like task balancing or time management.
- **Observe processes in real-time:** Leaders can obtain a practical understanding of workflows, tools, and cooperation dynamics by shadowing team members

or attending regular team meetings. This gives them personal knowledge of areas that require improvement.

Determining Baseline measurements: Determining baseline measurements is essential to comprehending performance as it stands today and assessing the effects of any upcoming adjustments. By monitoring KPIs and finding areas where adjustments could result in significant benefits, leaders can assess the efficiency of their processes.

Key performance indicators (KPIs) should be defined as follows:

- KPIs would include error rates, turnaround times, customer satisfaction ratings, or project completion rates, depending on the team's function. The performance levels as of right now are clearly depicted by these measurements.
- It may be necessary to establish distinct metrics for every operational procedure. For example, a marketing team may monitor the quantity of campaigns that are effectively carried out, whereas

an operations team may concentrate on the time required to finish particular activities.
- To make sure that any modifications that are made are producing the desired results, use the baseline metrics to establish targets that can be tracked over time.

8.2 Simplifying the Process

Simplifying workflow is crucial to establishing a productive, orderly team atmosphere. Leaders make sure that team members may concentrate on their most valuable activities by streamlining tasks and getting rid of unnecessary stages.

Identifying Redundancies and Bottlenecks: Leaders should examine every procedure to find processes that are superfluous, redundant, or resource drains that reduce output.
- **Remove redundant duties:** Roles and responsibilities may overlap in larger teams. To stop team members from working on the same tasks twice, leaders should assign distinct responsibilities

and explicitly define roles.

- **Automate processes that are repeated**: Team members can devote more time to strategic work when administrative duties, such as data input or reporting, are automated. Routine communications can be streamlined, for example, by utilizing customer relationship management (CRM) technologies or automating reporting.
- **Reduce approval bottlenecks:** Team productivity may suffer when decisions or initiatives need several approvals. By eliminating needless oversight or giving team members decision-making ability, leaders may frequently speed up operations.

Improving Communication Channels: Streamlined workflows, particularly in teams with intricate, interconnected activities, depend on clear and constant communication.

- **Use centralized communication technologies:** Project management software, Microsoft Teams, Slack, and other platforms keep communication accessible and organized for all team members, enabling real-time project progress updates.

- **Define standards for communication:** Establishing rules for when to use chat messages, emails, and in-person meetings guarantees effective communication that is suitable for the complexity or urgency of the message.
- **Promote openness and transparency:** Projects stay on schedule and misconceptions are decreased when team members have an open culture where they may easily discuss updates or possible problems.

Setting High-Value projects as a Priority: Team leaders can increase productivity by making sure that members dedicate their time to projects that directly support the organization's or team's strategic goals.

- **Use prioritizing frameworks:** Techniques like the Pareto Principle (concentrating on the 20% of tasks that generate 80% of results) or the Eisenhower Matrix (classifying tasks according to priority and urgency) assist teams in concentrating on work that has an impact.
- By assigning routine, lower-priority work to support personnel or automating them, you can empower team members to accept responsibility for

higher-impact duties.

- **Get rid of low-value activities**: Assess recurrent tasks to see if they can be phased out without impacting team performance or if they are necessary.

8.3 Putting Process Improvements into Practice

Leaders should concentrate on putting strategic improvements into place after identifying inefficiencies and creating efficient operations. Innovation and stability must be balanced for implementation to be successful, making sure that adjustments boost output without interfering with team operations.

Starting with Small, Manageable Changes: By implementing changes gradually, the team is kept from becoming overwhelmed and transitional times are made easier.

- **Introduce incremental changes:** Make minor tweaks that complement existing workflows rather than completely revamping a process. For instance, rather than reorganizing the entire report structure, start by streamlining certain components if the reporting process takes a long time.

- Piloting new procedures: Before scaling up, test changes on lower-stakes projects or with a smaller portion of the team to assess the impact. This strategy reduces hazards and offers information for improving modifications.
- **Get input at every step:** Before widespread adoption, problems can be avoided and changes can be made by encouraging team members to contribute their ideas and experiences throughout the implementation stage.

Measuring Impact and Adjusting Accordingly: Continuous evaluation is necessary for process improvements to be effective. To make sure they're reaching objectives, leaders should monitor changes and make appropriate adjustments to procedures using baseline metrics that have been set.

- Keep an eye on KPIs: Examine performance metrics on a regular basis to see if the adjustments are producing the anticipated gains. This could include increased client satisfaction, decreased error rates, or quicker project completion times.

- **Set up recurring review sessions:** Formal chances to address process improvements and collect team insights are offered by quarterly reviews or team check-ins.
- **Remain adaptable:** Not every modification will be successful. To ensure continual improvement, leaders should be willing to modify procedures in response to performance data and feedback.

Ensuring Team Buy-In: When the team is supportive and involved, process changes work best. By including team members in the process and explaining the reasoning behind each change, leaders may gain buy-in.

- **Explain the goal and advantages:** Describe the need for the adjustments and how they will help the team and the company. Team members might be encouraged to embrace new procedures by emphasizing how these enhancements lessen workloads, simplify duties, or boost productivity.
- Involve team members in the process of making decisions. Leaders can encourage a sense of ownership and dedication to the new procedures by using team feedback.

- **Offer assistance and training:** It's crucial to make sure team members feel supported throughout the shift and know how to apply new workflows. The transition time might be facilitated by documentation, training sessions, or one-on-one counseling.

Leaders may foster a collaborative, efficient, and strategically aligned team environment with company goals by implementing a systematic approach to process improvement. Leaders provide a strong foundation for long-term success by establishing clear expectations, encouraging candid communication, and enacting small but significant changes over time.

CHAPTER 9

Establishing a Powerful Individual Brand

Effective leadership requires developing a strong personal brand. A leader's principles, style, abilities, and reputation inside the company are all reflected in their brand. This brand influences the leader's capacity to motivate, sway, and accomplish goals in addition to how others view them. Leaders may create a brand that is genuine, respected, and in line with their organization's objectives by building credibility, demonstrating their leadership abilities, and regularly evaluating themselves.

9.1 Building Trustworthiness

Since credibility fosters the trust required for effective leadership, it is the foundation of a great personal brand. Even the most gifted leaders may find it difficult to win over their team, peers, and superiors if they lack credibility. To establish credibility, one must exhibit expertise, consistency, and transparency.

A credible leader demonstrates consistency in communication, behavior, and decision-making. Setting clear standards and creating a stable environment for team members are two benefits of acting consistently.

- **Keep your word:** Credibility is absolutely dependent on reliability. Leaders who regularly deliver on their commitments establish a reputation for reliability. This entails staying within commitment limits, fulfilling commitments, and meeting deadlines.
- **Set a steady example:** Team leaders ought to act as they would like to be treated. The culture of the team will automatically adopt the leader's values of integrity, teamwork, and punctuality.

Transparent leaders foster an environment of openness, which is essential for fostering trust and bringing teams together. Openly sharing the reasoning behind choices and being forthright about difficulties, achievements, and areas in need of development are all components of transparency.

- In order to be authentic, one must be honest about

both accomplishments and difficulties. Leaders encourage cooperation, trust, and creative solutions by admitting problems.

- **Explain decision-making processes:** Leaders show respect for their team's knowledge and opinions when they explain the rationale behind their choices. Teams may be more open to new ideas and efforts as a result of this transparency.

To preserve respect within the team, leaders must continuously exhibit and update their expertise and abilities. This covers both their field-specific technical capabilities and critical leadership competencies like strategic planning and dispute resolution.

- **Remain current with industry trends:** Credibility depends on staying up to date on tools, best practices, and advances in the business. This can entail reading and networking to keep current, attending workshops, or joining industry groups.
- **Continually improve your leadership skills:** Leaders who are dedicated to their own development indicate that they take their responsibilities seriously. A leader can maintain credibility and flexibility by

consistently improving their communication, delegating, and strategic planning abilities.

9.2 Highlighting Capabilities in Leadership

Aligning one's special traits with the demands of the group and the company is the key to demonstrating leadership strengths. Every leader contributes a unique combination of abilities, viewpoints, and experiences, and emphasizing these assets strategically aids in creating a powerful and genuine personal brand.

Effective leaders are self-aware of their greatest assets and how they complement the objectives of their teams and organizations.

- **Conduct a strengths assessment:** A leader's strengths can be revealed through the use of tools like the Myers-Briggs, CliftonStrengths, and other personality and strengths assessments. These tests assist leaders in recognizing their communication, problem-solving, and relationship-building inclinations and strengths.
- **Reflect on past successes:** Analyzing prior projects

or initiatives that were successful can reveal recurrent strengths like empathy, flexibility, or strategic thinking.

Align Strengths with Organizational Needs: When leaders match their special strengths with the goals and culture of the company, they have the greatest possible impact.

- **Emphasize capabilities that address team challenges:** For example, a leader with organizational skills should highlight a team's need for project management direction in order to support team goals. In the same way, if the team needs a morale boost, a leader with great motivating skills should use them.
- Adapt strategy according to context: Leaders may need to highlight different capabilities in different contexts. Adaptability could be crucial in a fast-paced environment, but rigorous planning might be more beneficial in a structured one.

Explain Leadership Strengths: Sharing one's strengths in daily encounters and at important times, like team meetings or performance reviews, requires tactful, strategic sharing.

- **Incorporate strengths into feedback and discussions:** Leaders can use instances that highlight their strengths when providing advice or comments. A leader who is gifted at addressing problems creatively, for example, can use personal experiences to demonstrate strategies for conquering obstacles.
- **Assume positions or projects that showcase your strengths:** In addition to showcasing their abilities, leaders who look for opportunities that capitalize on their strengths make significant contributions to the group and company.

9.3 Regularly Assessing Yourself

Building an authentic and successful personal brand requires self-evaluation. Leaders can better understand their strengths, fix their deficiencies, and guarantee consistency with organizational values by reflecting on their performance on a regular basis.

Effective self-evaluation entails a methodical examination of one's most recent successes, difficulties, and potential growth areas.

- **Assess accomplishments and shortcomings:** Leaders can keep a realistic view of their skills and areas for improvement by evaluating recent projects to see what worked and what could have been done better.
- **Allocate time for regular reflection:** To examine their objectives, difficulties, and successes, leaders should plan regular reflection periods, whether they be monthly, quarterly, or yearly.

Seeking Constructive Feedback: Other people's opinions offer insightful outside viewpoints that enable leaders to identify blind spots and implement significant changes.

- **Ask peers and team members for their opinions:** Leaders can solicit input informally, one-on-one, or through formalized techniques like anonymous surveys.
- Leaders who demonstrate that they are open to constructive criticism and eager to make adjustments not only better themselves but also strengthen their credibility and genuineness.

- **Adjusting Based on Self-Assessment:** Leaders should be prepared to make changes in order to maintain alignment with their own objectives as well as those of the organization, based on their own self-evaluations and feedback.
- **Update personal goals and objectives:** Leaders may find that they need to modify their leadership style or concentrate on specific abilities in order to better adapt to changes within the team or company.
- **Embrace continual growth:** Growth-minded leaders are flexible, resilient, and receptive to new challenges. Building a personal brand is a continuous process, and leaders who practice self-improvement regularly increase the power and significance of their brand.

As a leader, developing a strong personal brand is a complex process that calls for self-awareness, intentionality, and a dedication to personal development. In addition to inspiring trust and respect, leaders also help to create a healthy, resilient, and productive corporate culture by building credibility, emphasizing individual capabilities, and regularly evaluating themselves.

CHAPTER 10

Long-Term Success Planning

Achieving short-term triumphs is not enough for long-term leadership success; one must also make a lasting impression that lasts beyond one's term. Establishing frameworks that support ongoing development, creating an atmosphere where early accomplishments are used to produce long-lasting outcomes, and leaving a legacy of greatness are all components of true leadership. By emphasizing maintaining early victories, fostering a culture of continual development, and leaving a leadership legacy, this chapter examines how leaders can prepare for long-term success.

10.1 Maintaining Initial Gains

Setting the tone and building confidence in a new leadership post require early victories. To guarantee that momentum is maintained and converted into long-term success, they must be fostered and expanded upon. Leaders that are able to turn these first successes into sustained successes create a solid basis for future expansion.

Celebrate Early Successes Without Complacency: Although it's important to acknowledge early victories, it's crucial that they don't breed complacency. These triumphs should be viewed by leaders as stepping stones rather than the end goal.

- **Recognize team contributions:** Give credit where credit is due and celebrate the team's accomplishments. Receiving praise from the public raises spirits and encourages pride in one's job.
- **Consider the lessons that have been learned:** Analyze the factors that made it successful. Was it the plan? The act of execution? The cooperation of the team? Gaining insight into the elements that contributed to success can help you duplicate those results in the future.

Create Scalable procedures from Early Wins: Leaders should determine which activities or procedures led to their early successes and figure out how to expand them.

Implementing particular techniques that may be extended across teams or functions is frequently the key to success.

- **Identify essential practices:** Whether it's a specific workflow, communication plan, or approach to problem-solving, identifying the fundamental practices that underlie early wins guarantees that they can be standardized and optimized throughout the company.
- **Create scalability frameworks**: Leaders provide a framework that can be modified and expanded by formalizing and documenting effective procedures. This makes it possible to succeed even when the amount of responsibility increases.

Build on Successes with Strategic Vision: Early victories need to be connected to a larger vision in order to guarantee that they result in long-term benefits.

- **Align early wins with long-term goals**: Leaders should make sure that the organization's overall strategic objectives are directly linked to the early successes. This alignment gives future efforts direction and reaffirms the goal of the victories.
- Instead of aiming for a rapid string of victories,

leaders should concentrate on accomplishments that offer long-term benefits, including improved customer happiness, staff development, or process enhancements.

10.2 Establishing a Framework for Continuous Improvement

Leaders need to develop a culture of continual improvement in their teams if they want to plan for long-term success. Organizations must be dedicated to ongoing learning, development, and adaptation if they want to remain inventive, competitive, and responsive. Systems and structures that support continuous improvement and improve performance at all levels should be established by leaders.

Support a Growth Mindset: Leaders ought to support a mindset that places an emphasis on learning and development rather than stagnant performance.
- **Lead by example:** Leaders that show a dedication to learning, whether via professional development, learning new skills, or keeping up with industry

trends, provide a strong example for their people. Others are inspired to take charge of their own development as a result.
- **Create a safe space for failure:** When workers are free to try new things, take chances, and learn from their failures without worrying about consequences, a growth mindset flourishes.

Install Feedback Loops: A continuous cycle of feedback that can direct teams toward improved performance is necessary for continuous improvement. Leaders need to promote open communication and put in place systems for frequent feedback.
- **360-degree feedback:** Encourage staff members to give feedback to peers as well as leaders. A greater comprehension of team dynamics and areas for development is made possible by this holistic viewpoint.
- **Continuous evaluations of performance:** Growth and development, not only performance evaluation, should be the main focus of these reviews. Leaders should support staff members in setting goals for their own personal growth and monitoring their

progress while providing helpful criticism.

Support Innovation: Focusing on creativity and innovation is just as important to continuous improvement as process optimization.

- **Creative problem-solving:** Leaders should inspire their staff to think creatively and tackle problems from novel angles. This could entail setting up time and space for brainstorming sessions, funding R&D, or investigating novel technological advancements.
- **Reward creative concepts:** Teams are inspired to think creatively and strive for improvements in their job when innovation is acknowledged and rewarded, whether formally or informally.

Implement Systems for Ongoing Evaluation: Clearly defining procedures for evaluating performance and progress guarantees that everyday activities incorporate ongoing development.

- Key performance indicators, or KPIs, are as follows: Establish quantifiable KPIs in line with your long- and short-term objectives. These must be examined frequently in order to spot problem areas and make

the required corrections.
- **Audits of processes:** Regular audits of important procedures might reveal bottlenecks, inefficiencies, or areas for improvement.

10.3 Creating a Leadership Legacy

The culture a leader leaves behind is just as important as the accomplishments they make while in office. Building a culture of excellence, teamwork, and responsibility that endures beyond any one person is essential to leaving a leadership legacy.

Culture of Excellence: Leaders should work to establish a high-performance culture where continual improvement is expected and excellence is the norm.
- **Clearly define expectations:** Set quantifiable, unambiguous standards of excellence and share them with the team as a whole. Reiterate these ideals in every choice you make and action you take.
- **Offer chances for skill improvement:** Leaders that support their staff's development create a team that can continue to deliver high-caliber work. This

guarantees that the team culture will continue to value excellence long after the leader has left.

The ability of a leader to cultivate and guide future leaders who can carry on the mission and propel the organization's success is one of the most important components of their legacy.

- **Mentorship programs:** Leaders should actively guide, assist, and provide chances for growth to aspiring leaders. Either official mentorship programs or casual one-on-one coaching sessions may be used for this.
- Encourage staff members to assume leadership positions: Give team members the chance to take charge of tasks, make choices, and hone their leadership abilities. This guarantees the continuation of capable leadership in addition to aiding in the organization's growth.

Embed Values in Organizational DNA: A leadership legacy has the greatest influence when it is ingrained in the organization's principles and procedures. Long after a leader departs, the organization should still be guided by the principles they promoted.

- **Explain fundamental principles:** Make that the organization's basic values are communicated clearly and incorporated into strategy, decision-making, and day-to-day operations. These principles ought to direct behavior and influence society.
- **Support diversity and inclusion:** A leadership legacy should foster an environment where everyone is treated with respect and included. Leaders who cultivate diversity make sure that the company is flexible and sensitive to new concepts and shifting conditions.

Assure Organizational Resilience: Leaders should endeavor to make sure that the organization is resilient, able to overcome obstacles and carry on prospering without them.

- **Create a strong succession plan:** Make plans for leadership changes to prevent disruption in the organization when important leaders depart. Finding and training high-potential staff members to assume leadership positions is known as succession planning.

- **Create strong teams:** Cohesive, well-developed teams are the foundation of resilient enterprises. By emphasizing cooperation and team building, executives make sure the company has the tools and capacity to handle future difficulties.

Long-term success planning involves more than just achieving personal goals; it also entails developing enduring systems, cultures, and practices. Leaders make sure that their influence extends beyond short-term outcomes by maintaining early victories, putting in place frameworks for continuous improvement, and leaving a leadership legacy. Long beyond their direct engagement, the organization will continue to be shaped by their strong leadership, providing a basis for further growth and quality.

ABOUT THE AUTHOR

Renowned business strategist, author, and consultant James Royce Smartman has over twenty years of experience in a variety of fields, including corporate management, entrepreneurship, and finance. James has a strong academic background and an MBA from a prestigious university. As a result, he has a good understanding of the nuances of contemporary business practices and market dynamics.

James has held executive positions in multiple Fortune 500 businesses over his career, effectively leading projects that have sparked efficiency, growth, and innovation. Because of his special combination of theoretical knowledge and real-world experience, he can offer organizations of all sizes frameworks and concrete tactics.

James is regularly asked to speak at conferences and seminars as a thought leader in the business sector, offering his knowledge on subjects including strategic planning, organizational behavior, and leadership development. In addition, he frequently contributes his thoughts on new trends and best practices to eminent business journals.

James Royce Smartman is devoted to helping company executives and entrepreneurs realize their objectives by providing them with creative solutions and useful guidance. His writings seek to demystify difficult business ideas so that readers of all skill levels can understand and use them. James offers a road map for success that is in line with the changing business environment of today by emphasizing practical examples and tried-and-true tactics.

James regularly mentors young professionals and supports different business projects that foster entrepreneurship and innovation in addition to his writing and consulting work. He promotes an organizational culture that welcomes change and encourages expansion because he believes in the value of teamwork and ongoing education.

www.ingramcontent.com/pod-product-compliance
Lightning Source LLC
Chambersburg PA
CBHW070422240526
45472CB00020B/1141